TABLE OF CONTENTS

For the Teacher

This reproducible study guide to use in conjunction with a specific novel consists of lessons for guided reading. Written in chapter-by-chapter format, the guide contains a synopsis, pre-reading activities, vocabulary and comprehension exercises, as well as extension activities to be used as follow-up to the novel.

In a homogeneous classroom, whole class instruction with one title is appropriate. In a heterogeneous classroom, reading groups should be formed: each group works on a different novel on its reading level. Depending upon the length of time devoted to reading in the classroom, each novel, with its guide and accompanying lessons, may be completed in three to six weeks.

Begin using NOVEL-TIES for reading development by distributing the novel and a folder to each child. Distribute duplicated pages of the study guide for students to place in their folders. After examining the cover and glancing through the book, students can participate in several pre-reading activities. Vocabulary questions should be considered prior to reading a chapter; all other work should be done after the chapter has been read. Comprehension questions can be answered orally or in writing. The classroom teacher should determine the amount of work to be assigned, always keeping in mind that readers must be nurtured and that the ultimate goal is encouraging students' love of reading.

The benefits of using NOVEL-TIES are numerous. Students read good literature in the original, rather than in abridged or edited form. The good reading habits, formed by practice in focusing on interpretive comprehension and literary techniques, will be transferred to the books students read independently. Passive readers become active, avid readers.

SYNOPSIS

Dinosaurs Before Dark, the first book in the *Magic Tree House* series, is the story of two children who climb up to a tree house and experience adventures with dinosaurs in the prehistoric past.

While Annie and her older brother Jack are playing in the woods near their home, Annie, who is the more adventurous of the two, climbs a rope ladder and discovers a tree house that is stocked with books. Because he loves books, Jack is persuaded to join her. As the children are looking at a book about dinosaurs, Jack sees a picture of a Pteranodon, an ancient flying reptile. He whispers, "I wish I could see a Pteranodon for real."

No sooner has he expressed his desire when they notice a live Pteranodon flying toward the tree house. The tree house starts spinning, and continues faster and faster. When it stops, Annie and Jack find themselves in the world of the book that Jack is holding. They approach the Pteranodon, who appears to be friendly. Jack records this experience in the notebook he carries with him.

Next, they encounter a Triceratops at the top of the hill. Jack studies it and again takes notes. As they wander through the valley, Jack discovers a medallion in the grass, suggesting that someone has been there before them.

Continuing on, they meet a giant duck-billed dinosaur mother, an Anatosaurus, and see nests filled with baby dinosaurs. When a threatening Tyrannosaurus rex approaches Jack, the Pteranodon rescues him temporarily by flying him back to the tree house. As the Tyrannosaurus rex nears them, Jack finds the book about Pennsylvania, points to the picture of the woods near their home, and shouts, "I wish we could go home!" The tree house spins, and when it stops, they are home.

The children discover that real time has not passed since they left. They wonder if the trip to dinosaur time has been a dream. But, as Jack clasps the gold medallion in his pocket, he is sure that their adventure has been real. The children decide to climb up to the tree house again the next day.

PRE-READING ACTIVITIES

1. Preview the book by reading the title and the author's name and by looking at the picture on the cover of the book. What do you think the book will be about? Do you think the events will be real or make-believe?

2. This is the first book in the *Magic Tree House* series. Have you read any other books in this series? If you have, what is the same in all of the books?

3. Brainstorm with your classmates to tell all you know about each of the following kinds of dinosaurs. Write this information in the chart below. As you read the book, correct any mistakes and add new information.

	What I Know	**What I Learned**
Pteranodon	*They fly*	
Triceratops	*They have 3 horns*	
Anatosaurus		
Tyrannosaurus rex	*They're the largest carnivore*	

4. Read the Table of the Contents at the beginning of the book. Use the clues in the chapter titles to make five predictions about what will happen in the story. After you have finished reading the book, return to your predictions and see if any of them did happen.

5. Look at the story map on page three of this study guide. Fill it in as you read the book. After you finish reading, compare your story map to those of your classmates.

STORY MAP

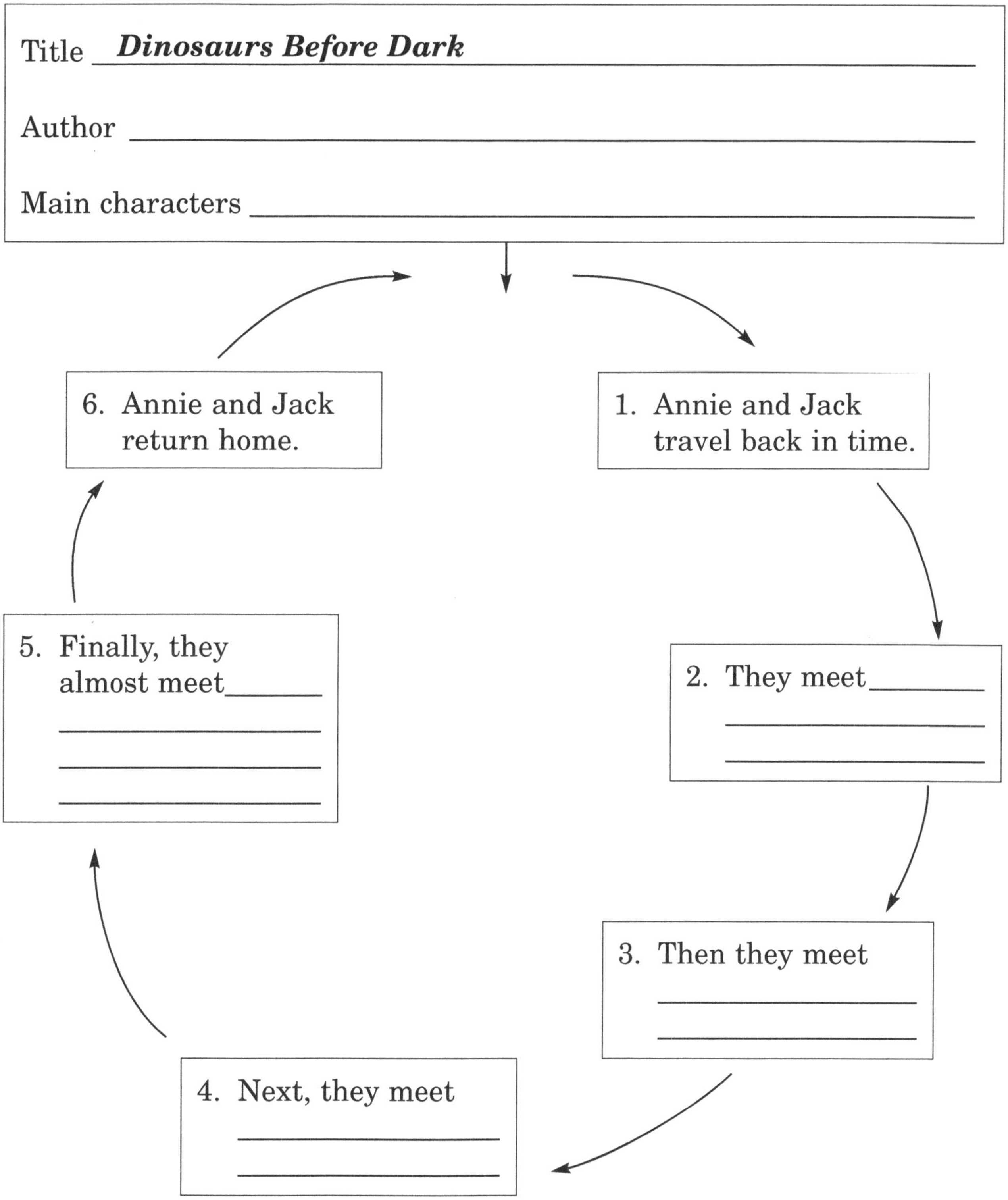

Title ___*Dinosaurs Before Dark*___________________

Author ___________________________________

Main characters ___________________________

6. Annie and Jack return home.

1. Annie and Jack travel back in time.

5. Finally, they almost meet________
____
____
____

2. They meet________
____
____

4. Next, they meet
____
____

3. Then they meet
____
____

CHAPTER 1

Vocabulary: Use the sentences to help you figure out the meanings of the underlined words. Then draw a line from each word on the left to its meaning on the right.

- I will <u>whisper</u> so that I do not bother the people who are reading.

- It is fun to wear a costume and <u>pretend</u> that you are a lion.

- The rabbit <u>disappeared</u> in the bushes and could not be found.

- It was hard to find the birthday card because it was <u>tucked</u> between the pages of the book.

1. whisper
2. pretend
3. disappeared
4. tucked

a. put in a tight, hidden place
b. make believe
c. speak very softly
d. went out of sight

> Read to find out what the children discover in the woods.

Questions:

1. Why does Annie say "Help! A monster?"

2. Why does Jack keep calling Annie and telling her it is time to go home?

3. Why does Jack finally decide to go up into the tree house?

Questions for Discussion:

1. How does Jack feel about spending time with his younger sister?

2. What do you think will happen to the children in the tree house?

Chapter 1 (cont.)

Graphic Organizer: Character

Use the Venn diagram below to compare Annie and Jack. Write about the ways they are the same in the overlapping part of the circles. Add more information as you continue to read the story.

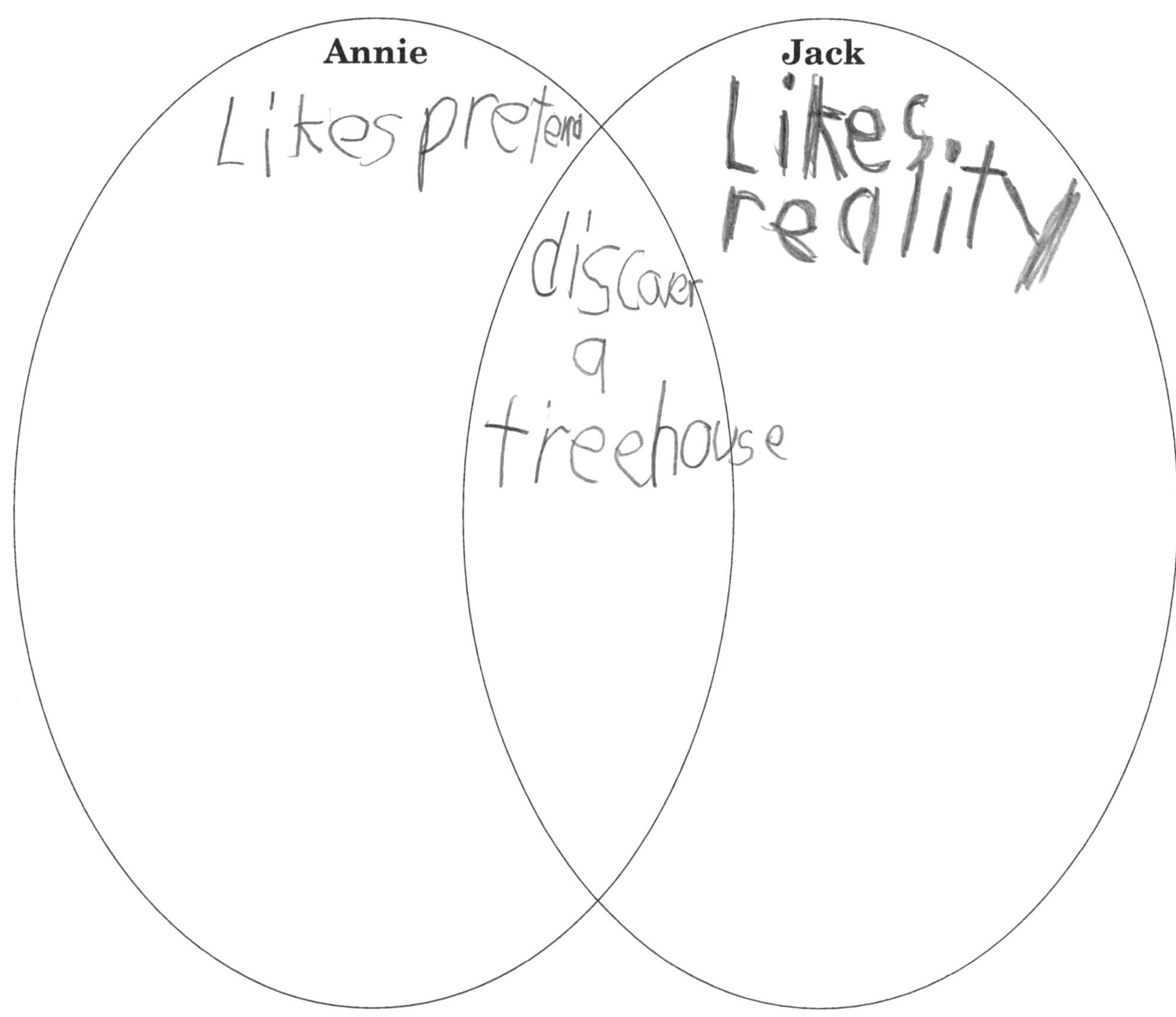

Writing Activity:

Write about a real or imagined time when you made an interesting discovery. Tell what you saw and what you did.

CHAPTERS 2, 3

Vocabulary: Use the words in the Word Box and the clues below to complete this crossword puzzle.

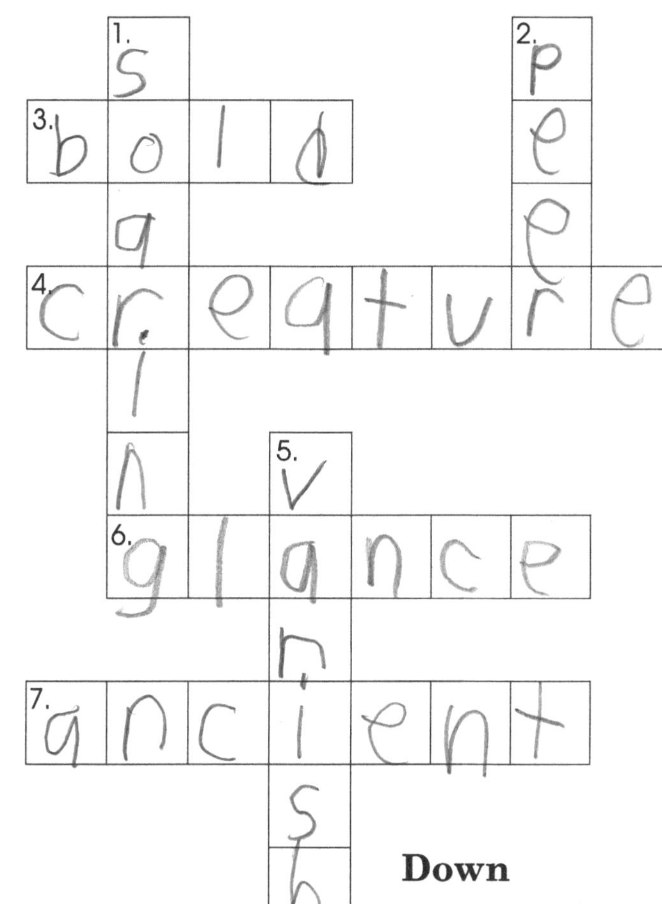

Across

3. without fear
4. a living being, especially an animal
6. look quickly
7. very old

Down

1. flying high in the air
2. look at carefully in order to see clearly
5. disappear; stop being

Read to find out what happens in the tree house.

Questions:

1. Why is Jack interested in a book about Pennsylvania?
2. What happens when Jack wishes he could see a Pteranodon?

Chapters 2,3 (cont.)

3. What magical things happen in the tree house?

4. What looks different in the land of the Pteranodon?

5. How do the children know *when* they have landed?

Questions for Discussion:

1. Why do you think Annie gives Jack a book about dinosaurs?

2. How would you answer Annie's question, "Where is here?"

3. What do you think will happen when Annie walks up to the Pteranodon?

Science Connection:

In Chapter two the children meet a Pteranodon. Using information from the book, encyclopedias, and books about dinosaurs, fill in the chart on the next page. Draw a picture of a Pteranodon.

 ### Writing Activity:

Pretend you are Annie or Jack. Begin a journal entry telling your thoughts and feelings on the day you meet a Pteranodon.

PTERANODON

When it Lived	
How Big it Was	
What it Ate	
Other Interesting Facts	
How it Looked	

CHAPTER 4

Vocabulary: Read each sentence. Use the meaning of the whole sentence to help you figure out the meaning of each underlined word. Write your definition. Then check your definition with a dictionary.

1. The girl was <u>alert</u> and quickly pulled her baby sister away from the hot stove.

   Your definition ___________________________________

   Dictionary definition_______________________________

2. The bird had a strange <u>crest</u> on top of its head.

   Your definition ___________________________________

   Dictionary definition_______________________________

3. You should be very <u>cautious</u> when you cross the busy street.

   Your definition ___________________________________

   Dictionary definition_______________________________

4. <u>Scientists</u> are working hard to find cures for many diseases.

   Your definition ___________________________________

   Dictionary definition_______________________________

5. Because the animal looked different from the others, we thought it could have been a <u>mutant</u>.

   Your definition ___________________________________

   Dictionary definition_______________________________

> Read to find out more about the Pteranodon.

Questions:

1. How does Annie try to make friends with the dinosaur?
2. Why does Jack decide that he, too, will go down to examine the creature?
3. Why does Jack take notes about the Pteranodon?

Chapter 4 (cont.)

Questions for Discussion:

1. How do you think the Pteranodon would answer Annie's questions, "Did we come to a time long ago?" and "Is this the place from long ago?"

2. What kind of dinosaur do you think is standing on the hill?

3. Do you think the children are in danger?

Word Study: Adjectives

Adjectives are words that describe. They are words such as *kind, terrible,* and *pretty.* Write as many adjectives as you can find to describe "Henry."

____

____

____

____

____

____

Literature Study: Dialogue

Annie and Jack have different opinions about the Pteranodon. Put a check [✔] below the character who made each statement. Check in the book to see if you are right.

	Annie	Jack
His brain's probably no bigger than a bean.		
No. He's very smart. I can feel it.		
Maybe he's a mutant.		
He's no mutant.		

Chapter 4 (cont.)

Literary Device: Simile

A simile is a comparison of one thing to another, using the words "like" or "as." The following sentence is a simile: "The Pteranodon's long jaws were opening and closing like a pair of scissors." This is a simile because the jaws are being compared to scissors, using the word "like."

Write a simile by completing each of the following sentences. The first one has been done for you.

1. The cloud was like ___a puffy pillow_________________.

2. The hot sun was like _____________________________.

3. The gentle breeze was like _________________________.

4. The falling snow was like __________________________.

5. The lion's roar was like ___________________________.

Science Connection:

In Chapter Four you learned additional facts about the Pteranodon. Add these to the Pteranodon page in your science folder.

Writing Activity:

Finish Annie's or Jack's journal entry that you began for Chapters Two and Three.

CHAPTERS 5, 6

Vocabulary: Draw a line from each word on the left to its meaning on the right. Then use the numbered words to fill in the blanks in the sentences below.

1.	clutch	a.	loud, sharp sound
2.	incredible	b.	shut with force
3.	slam	c.	push gently
4.	nudge	d.	sparkle brightly
5.	glitter	e.	hold tightly
6.	medallion	f.	large medal
7.	shriek	g.	unbelievable

1. She heard the door _________________ shut as he rushed out of the room.

2. His prize for winning the race was a beautiful _________________.

3. You could see stars _________________ from far away.

4. It was _________________ to see an animal as big as a two-story building.

5. She gave him a _________________ to wake him.

6. He ran to help his sister when he heard her _________________ .

7. I _________________ my hat to keep it from blowing away in the wind.

> Read to find out about the huge dinosaur on top of the hill.

Questions:

1. How does Jack know that the new dinosaur is a Triceratops?

2. Why do Annie and Jack decide to go to see the Triceratops?

Chapters 5, 6 (cont.)

3. Why does Annie shriek?

4. Why does Jack tell Annie to pretend to chew?

5. Why does the Anatosaurus follow Annie up the hill?

6. Why does the Anatosaurus suddenly run away?

Questions for Discussion:

1. Why does Annie believe that the Triceratops is nice?

2. Why does Jack believe that someone was there before them?

3. Why do you think the Anatosaurus waves her arms at Annie as she walks near the nests?

Word Study: Compound Words

A compound word is made up of two or more words. Draw a line from each word in column A to a word in column B. Write the compound word on the line.

A	B	Compound Words
1. hill	pack	_________________
2. back	book	_________________
3. some	top	_________________
4. note	mark	_________________
5. book	thing	_________________

Write a sentence for each compound word.

Chapters 5, 6 (cont.)

Literature Study: Tone and Mood

Reread the last page of Chapter Six. How does the author want you to feel as you read this page? Write some words and phrases the author uses to make you feel this way.

____

____

____

____

Science Connections:

1. On the following two pages of this study guide, there are questions about the Triceratops and Anatosaurus. Draw pictures of these dinosaurs. Using information from the book, encyclopedias, and books about dinosaurs, fill in the charts. Put the pages in your dinosaur folder.

2. What animals alive today hatch from eggs as dinosaurs did in the past? What does this tell you about dinosaurs?

Writing Activity:

Jack has mixed feelings about his sister Annie. When Annie disappears down the hill, Jack is very angry with her and says, "I'm going to kill her." But when Annie shrieks and calls for him to come, Jack runs and saves Annie

Write about a time when you had mixed feelings about someone or something. Explain how you felt and what you did.

TRICERATOPS

When it Lived	
How Big it Was	
What it Ate	
Other Interesting Facts	
How it Looked	

ANATOSAURUS

When it Lived	
How Big it Was	
What it Ate	
Other Interesting Facts	
How it Looked	

CHAPTERS 7, 8

Vocabulary: Many words in the English language have more than one meaning. Write the letter of the definition that best fits the underlined word in each of the sentences below.

1. The ball did not hit Bill because he was able to <u>duck</u> quickly.

   a. a swimming bird   b. lower the head or body suddenly

2. She was angry and <u>left</u> without saying a word.

   a. went away   b. side or direction

3. We could see the ship because it was sailing near the <u>coast</u>.

   a. ride or slide down a hill   b. land along the sea

4. He used a <u>scoop</u> to dig up some sand.

   a. tool like a shovel   b. act of taking up

5. Our team was able to <u>beat</u> your team because we had faster runners.

   a. win against   b. hit again and again

> Read to learn about the next dinosaur the children meet.

Questions:

1. Why does Annie remind Jack about the dinosaur book?

2. Why does Jack go back to the hill to get the book and his backpack?

3. Why can't Jack get back to the tree house after he has his book and backpack?

4. Why does Jack think that the dinosaur book is no help at all?

5. Why is the ground shaking?

Chapters 7, 8 (cont.)

Questions for Discussion:

1. Why do you think Jack's wishes aren't working now?

2. What are Jack's choices when he sees Tyrannosaurus rex coming toward the hill? If you had to make a choice, what would you do?

Science Connection:

Using information from the book, encyclopedias, and books about dinosaurs, fill in the chart for a Tyrannosaurus rex. Draw a picture. Put the page in your dinosaur folder.

Writing Activity:

Write a short paragraph to tell what you think will happen when the Tyrannosaurus rex meets Annie and Jack.

TYRANNOSAURUS REX

When it Lived	
How Big it Was	
What it Ate	
Other Interesting Facts	
How it Looked	

CHAPTERS 9, 10

Vocabulary: Read each group of words. Choose the one word that does not belong with the others and cross it out. On the line below the words, tell how the rest of the words are alike.

1. race   chomp   chew   bite

   These words are alike because___________________________________

   ____

2. amaze   refuse   surprise   astonish

   These words are alike because___________________________________

   ____

3. wobble   shake   tremble   sleep

   These words are alike because___________________________________

   ____

4. still   dirty   quiet   calm

   These words are alike because___________________________________

   ____

> Read to find out how Annie and Jack try to return home.

Questions:

1. Why does Jack climb aboard the Pteranodon?

2. Why does Jack thank Annie for saving his life?

3. Why does Jack have to find the book about Pennsylvania?

4. After they arrive home, how do the children know that no time has passed since they left on their adventure?

Chapters 9, 10 (cont.)

5. Why do Annie and Jack decide not to tell anyone about their adventure?

6. At the end of the story, why is Jack sure that their trip in the magic tree house has been real?

Questions for Discussion:

1. Why do you think the Pteranodon was helpful to Jack?

2. What do you think the letter M stands for on the medallion?

3. Will the children return to the tree house? What makes you think as you do?

Cause and Effect:

Complete the following sentences:

1. Jack climbed onto the Pteranodon's back because_______________________

____

____

2. Jack climbed quickly into the tree house because___________________

____

____

3. Jack and Annie knew they were home because _____________________

____

____

Chapters 9, 10 (cont.)

Graphic Organizer: Sequence

Jack and Annie met four dinosaurs. In the boxes below, write the name of each dinosaur in the order in which they met it.

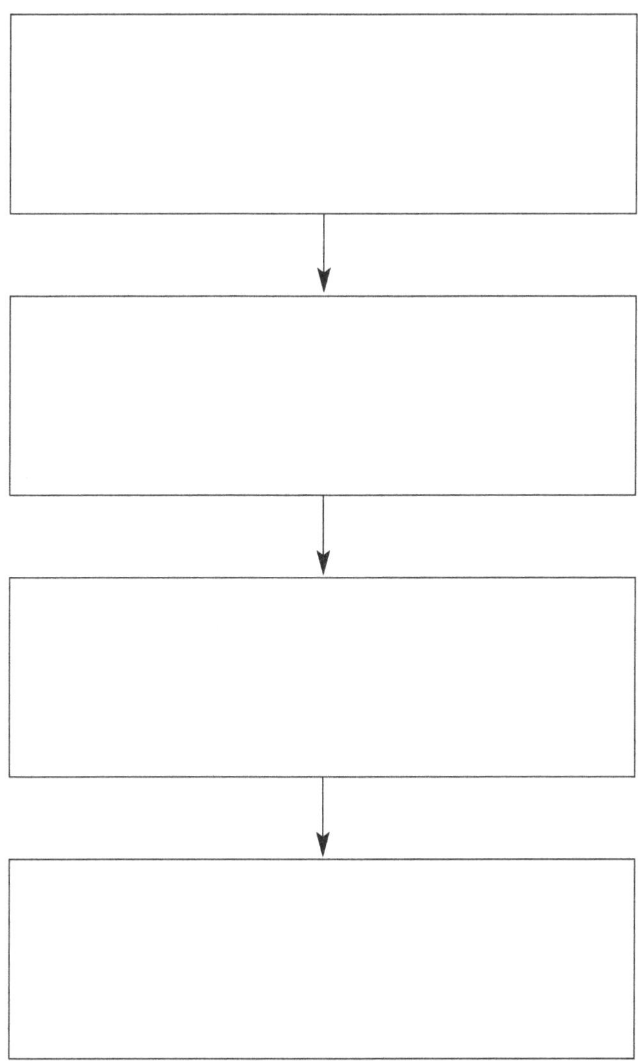

Writing Activity:

Make up a story to tell what will happen the next time the children visit the tree house.

CLOZE ACTIVITY

The following passage is taken from Chapter Nine of the book. Read the entire passage before filling in the blanks. Then reread the passage and fill in each blank with a word that makes sense. Finally, you may compare your words with those of the author.

It was amazing! It was a _______________![1]

Jack felt like a bird. As light as a _______________.[2]

The wind was rushing through his _______________.[3] The air smelled sweet and fresh.

He _______________.[4] He laughed.

Jack couldn't believe it. He was _______________[5] on the back of an ancient flying _______________![6]

The Pteranodon sailed over the stream, over the _______________[7] and bushes.

Then he carried Jack down to the _______________[8] of the oak tree.

When they came to a _______________,[9] Jack slid off the creature's back. And _______________[10] on the ground.

Then the _______________[11] took off again and glided into the _______________.[12]

"Bye, Henry," whispered Jack.

"Are you okay?" _______________[13] shouted from the tree house.

Jack pushed his _______________[14] into place. He kept staring up at the _______________.[15]

"Jack, are you okay?" Annie called.

Jack _______________[16] up at Annie. He smiled.

"Thanks for saving my life," he said. "That was really fun."

POST-READING ACTIVITIES

1. Return to the Story Map on page three of this study guide. Complete the map and then compare your map with those of your classmates.

2. Return to the chart on dinosaurs that you began in the Pre-Reading Activities on page two of this study guide. Correct any wrong information in the first column. Write what you learned about each dinosaur in the second column.

3. Return to the "Characters" diagram you began on page five of this study guide. Add more ways in which Annie and Jack were alike and different.

4. Why do you think this book was titled *Dinosaurs Before Dark*? Can you think of another title for the book?

5. With your classmates, paint a mural showing the dinosaurs and their surroundings.

6. Pretend that Annie and Jack take another trip in the magic tree house and find a new dinosaur that no one has ever seen. Give it a name and tell why you chose that name. Write a story about the adventures that Annie and Jack have with the new dinosaur.

7. Read another book in the *Magic Tree House* series. Compare it with *Dinosaurs Before Dark*. Are Annie and Jack still the main characters? What else is the same? What is different? Which book did you like better?

8. Look in newspapers and magazines to find articles about dinosaurs. Share them with your class, and add them to your dinosaur folder.

9. Play this word game with your classmates.
   - Write the name of one of the dinosaurs on the chalkboard.
   - Give each child a piece of paper.
   - Set a timer for ten minutes.
   - Everyone should try to find smaller words in the dinosaur's name.
   - Use only the letters in the name.
   - You may mix up letters and use letters more than once.
   - When the time is up, the person with the most words wins the game.

Post-Reading Activities (cont.)

10. **Science Connection:** Play this science game about dinosaurs with your classmates.

    Using the information you learned from the story and from your dinosaur folder, write five questions about dinosaurs.

    - Ask each of your classmates to write five questions about dinosaurs.
    - Cut them into strips, with one question on each strip.
    - Place each question in a basket.
    - Divide the class into two teams.
    - Children from each team take turns picking a question from the basket and answering it.
    - Each correct answer is one point.
    - After all the questions have been answered, the team with the most points wins the game.

SUGGESTIONS FOR FURTHER READING

Aliki. *Digging up Dinosaurs*. HarperCollins

Andrews, Roy Chapman. *In the Days of the Dinosaurs*. Random House

Benton, Dr. Michael. *The Dinosaur Encyclopedia*. Aladdin Books.

Clark, Mary Lou. *The True Book of Dinosaurs*. Children's Press.

Cole, Joanna. *Dinosaur Story*. Scholastic.

——————. *The Magic School Bus in the Time of Dinosaurs*. Scholastic.

Cole, Stephen. *Walking with Dinosaurs*. Dorling Kindersley.

Daly, Kathleen. *Dinosaurs*. Golden Press.

Eldridge, David. *Last of the Dinosaurs*. Troll.

Gibbons, Gail. *Dinosaurs*. Scholastic.

Harrison, Carol. *Dinosaurs Everywhere*. Scholastic.

Lauder, Patricia. *The News About Dinosaurs*. Aladdin Books.

Packard, Mary. *Dinosaurs*. Simon & Schuster.

Selsam, Millicent. *Tyrannosaurus Rex*. HarperCollins.

Shields, Carol Diggory. *Saturday Night at the Dinosaur Stomp*. Scholastic.

Simon, Seymour. *New Questions and Answers About Dinosaurs*. HarperCollins.

Teitelbaum, Michael. *Dinosaurs of the Land, Sea and Air*. The Rourke Corp.

——————. *Dinosaurs of the Prehistoric Era*. The Rourke Corp.

Wood, A.J. *A Night in the Dinosaur Graveyard*. HarperCollins.

Some Other Titles in the *Magic Tree House* Series by Mary Pope Osborne

* *The Knight at Dawn*. (#2) Random House.

* *Mummies in the Morning*. (#3) Random House.

Pirates Past Noon. (#4) Random House.

Night of the Ninjas. (#5) Random House.

Afternoon on the Amazon. (#6) Random House.

Sunset of the Sabertooth. (#7) Random House.

* NOVEL-TIES Study Guides are available for these titles.

ANSWER KEY

Chapter 1

Vocabulary: 1. c 2. b 3. d 4. a

Questions: 1. Annie says "Help! A monster" because she loves to pretend. 2. Jack keeps calling Annie and telling her it is time to go home because the sun is about to set and it is almost dark. 3. Tempted by the books Annie discovers, Jack finally decides to go up into the tree house.

Chapters 2, 3

Vocabulary: Across—3. bold 4. creature 6. glance 7. ancient; Down—1. soaring 2. peer 5. vanish

Questions: 1. Jack is interested in a book about Pennsylvania because he lives in Frog Creek, Pennsylvania. 2. When Jack wishes he could see a Pteranodon, one appears outside the window. 3. Magically in the tree house, the world of the picture in the book becomes real and a Pteranodon appears to be standing at the base of the tree. 4. The place where Annie and Jack land has ground covered with ferns and tall grass. There is a winding stream, a sloping hill, and volcanoes rumbling in the distance. 5. The book about dinosaurs informs the children that Pteranodons became extinct about 65 million years ago, the time they assume they must have landed.

Chapter 4

Vocabulary: 1. alert—watchful; wide awake 2. crest—comb; tuft on the head of a bird or other animal 3. cautious—very careful 4. scientists—people who work in science 5. mutant—new plant or animal, formed by changes in that plant or animal

Questions: 1. To make friends with the dinosaur, Annie holds out her hand, touches the Pteranodon's crest, strokes his neck, and talks to it. 2. Jack decides that he, too, will go down to examine the creature because he believes that it would be good to take scientific notes. 3. Jack takes notes about the Pteranodon because he believes that he and Annie are probably the first people in the whole world to see a real, live Pteranodon.

Chapters 5, 6

Vocabulary: 1. e 2. g 3. b 4. c 5. d 6. f 7. a; 1. slam 2. medallion 3. glitter 4. incredible 5. nudge 6. shriek 7. clutch

Questions: 1. Jack knows that the new dinosaur is a Triceratops because he sees a picture of it in his dinosaur book. 2. Annie and Jack decide to go to see the Triceratops because they learn from the book that it does not eat meat, and because they are probably the first people in the whole world to ever see a real, live Triceratops. 3. Annie shrieks because a giant duck-billed dinosaur is standing over her while she is crouched next to a dinosaur nest. 4. Jack tells Annie to pretend to chew because he has read that you should do that if a mad dog comes at you, and the huge dinosaur is near Annie. 5. The Anatosaurus follows Annie up the hill because it likes to eat flowers, and Annie goes up the hill where there are more flowers. 6. The Anatosaurus suddenly runs away because it seems to be afraid of an enormous, ugly monster that is coming across the plain.

Word Study: Compound Words—1. hilltop 2. backpack 3. something 4. notebook 5. bookmark

Chapters 7, 8

Vocabulary: 1. b 2. a 3. b 4. a 5. a

Questions: 1. Annie reminds Jack about the dinosaur book because she wants to go home. She reasons that the book was instrumental in bringing them to this new place and should be able to bring them back. 2. Jack goes back to the hill to get his book and backpack because the book does not belong to him and he has to return it. Also, his notebook is in his backpack. 3. Jack is unable to return to the tree house after he has his book and his backpack because the Tyrannosaurus rex is standing between him and the tree house. 4. Jack thinks that the dinosaur book is no help at all because it does not give any information that would be helpful to him. It says that a Tyrannosaurus rex would eat a human in one bite. 5. The ground is shaking because the huge Tyrannosaurus rex is coming toward the hill.

Chapters 9, 10

Vocabulary:

1. race—the other words all describe a way of eating   2. refuse—the other words all describe a reaction to an unexpected event   3. sleep—the other words all describe a quivering motion   4. dirty—the other words all describe a situation that is free of motion or turbulence.

Questions:

1. Jack climbs aboard the Pteranodon because he fears the approaching Tyrannosaurus rex and wants to be flown out of harm's way. 2. Jack thanks Annie for saving his life because she showed the Pteranodon how to rescue him. 3. Jack has to find the book about Pennsylvania so that he can look at the picture of Frog Woods and make a wish to go home before the Tyrannosaurus rex attacks. 4. After they arrive home, the children know that no time has passed since they left on their adventure because it is still late afternoon, the sun is still about to set, and mom is still calling them. 5. Annie and Jack decide not to tell anyone about their adventure because they know that no one will believe their story. 6. At the end of the story, Jack is sure that their trip in the magic tree house has been real because in his pocket is the gold medallion that he found in the land of dinosaurs.